BEHIND THE BARAAT

The Silent Crises of Forced Choices and Marital Trauma in Modern India

MUSKAN SHARMA

Disclaimer: *The narratives, accounts, and case profiles presented in this book are composite studies drawn from contemporary legal and sociological patterns in Indian matrimonial disputes. To protect individual privacy and maintain strict confidentiality, all names, characters, professions, geographic locations, and identifying details have been completely anonymized or altered. Any resemblance to actual persons, living or dead, or actual events is purely coincidental. The legal discussions contained herein are intended for educational and social awareness purposes only and do not constitute formal legal advice.*

For every voice that was silenced,

and for those still finding the courage to speak.

About the Book

Behind the Baraat exposes the hidden trauma of forced matrimonial choices in modern India, revealing how rigid family criteria and social stigma shatter mental health and relationships across genders. Aimed at young adults, parents, legal professionals, and counsellors, it uncovers the psychological toll of coerced marriages, compatibility blind spots, in-law enmeshment, and weaponized laws. Through real case studies and reflective exercises, readers shift from Log Kya Kahenge compliance to empowered boundary-setting and intentional partnership. By the journey's end, individuals and families gain practical insights to protect mental well-being and foster respectful, compatible unions.

Contents

CHAPTER 1

The Coerced "I Do": Unveiling the Pressure Cooker

Tradition vs. Modernity: The Urgency Narrative

Imagine a timer counting down to your "ideal" wedding age: twenty-five for women, twenty-eight for men. In many families, those numbers are treated as deadlines. What begins as friendly advice, "When will you settle down?", quickly escalates into pressure: shame, threats, and relentless reminders. That pressure becomes coercion, not choice.

Modern life values personal growth and emotional intelligence (EQ): the capacity to understand one's own feelings and the feelings of others, and to use that awareness to make healthier choices. Most parents act from genuine love and deep concern for their children's futures. Yet that care can sometimes become entangled with social pressure, unmet hopes, or inherited ideas about what a good life looks like. When love and concern merge with those external pressures, boundaries can quietly collapse and personal autonomy can be lost.

Both men and women suffer under this urgency. Women may face dowry demands, social isolation, and blame if they resist. Men can face false legal accusations, public shaming, and extreme emotional pressure that leads to despair. This is not about individual weakness; it is about a system that prizes conformity over individual well-being.

Stories from the Margins

The following are composite, fully anonymized profiles reflecting patterns drawn from real experiences.

Case Study A, Anita, 26

Anita's family organized meeting after meeting with prospective grooms. Every rejection ended in anger.

Relatives began calling her "picky" and spread rumors about her character. Feeling trapped and ashamed, Anita agreed to a match. Within months, she fell into severe depression and began experiencing suicidal ideation.

Case Study B, Vikram, 29

Vikram wanted a partner he could genuinely connect with and declined several arranged matches for that reason. His parents threatened to cut him off, warning him of "what people will say." Pressured into agreement, he was later dragged into lengthy legal proceedings by false complaints from the other family. He became anxious, isolated, and unable to trust.

These stories reveal a recurring pattern: pressure leads to rushed decisions, which lead in turn to feelings of betrayal, trauma, or legal exposure. This is not individual failure; it is a matchmaking system that deploys shame and threat to override personal agency.

The Psychological Toll of Coercion

Being pushed into marriage leaves deep marks on mind and body. Common responses include:

- Anxiety and constant worry: a persistent sense of dread before each family confrontation.
- Depression and emotional numbness: joy fades and ordinary life feels hollow.
- PTSD FULL FORM Post-Traumatic Stress Disorder: nightmares, flashbacks, and triggers tied to the period of pressure.
- Eroded self-worth: a growing belief that one's own needs do not matter.
- Social withdrawal: suppressing one's pain to avoid the judgment of peers.

When families have not developed emotional communication tools, they may fall back on patterns of shame, gaslighting ("You are overreacting"), or stonewalling, not always out of malice, but often out of habit, fear, or the weight of their own conditioning. Over time, repeated exposure to these patterns rewires the stress response, making recovery harder even after the situation resolves.

Practical Language for Difficult Conversations

If you choose to speak up, calm and direct language reduces conflict. Consider these phrases:

- "I appreciate your concern, but this decision belongs to me."
- "I need time to reflect and make my own choice."
- "I feel anxious when I am rushed; I need to proceed at my own pace."
- "I hear you, but I cannot agree to this right now."

Rehearse these privately. They set boundaries without escalating tension.

Reflective Prompts

1. When did you first notice pressure to marry? Describe that moment in detail.
2. Who in your life reinforces the urgency narrative, and how do they do it?
3. Have you sacrificed something you valued to avoid family conflict or social shame? What was it?

---

4. Which response do you default to under pressure, people-pleasing, withdrawal, or anger?
5. What is one clear boundary you can set this week to protect your mental health?

A coerced "I do" rarely marks the beginning of a healthy life together. More often it initiates a long, concealed struggle: guilt, resentment, depression, or legal entanglement. Tradition becomes harmful when it displaces respect for individual choice.

Recognizing the pressure and naming its effects is the first step toward reclaiming agency. Start with small, private actions: honest reflection, one boundary, one trusted conversation.

Practical supports such as legal counsel, professional counselling, and trusted friendships can help you move from reactive compliance to deliberate choice.

CHAPTER 2

The Compatibility Blindspot: Beyond Status and Wealth

In many cultures, a good match is measured by salary, property, and family name: tangible assets that promise safety and social approval. But these metrics often obscure what matters most: how two people connect, communicate, and care for each other. This chapter examines why emotional intelligence and shared values are more reliable foundations for a lasting marriage than any balance sheet.

Section 1: The Traditional Metrics of Marital Value

Conventional marriage checklists typically include:

- High salary or business income
- Property ownership: land, flat, or family home
- Family reputation and social standing
- Matching caste or community background

These criteria feel reassuring because they are measurable. Yet they carry hidden risks:

- Wealth does not guarantee maturity, empathy, or respect.
- Property ownership creates a feeling of stability, but a secure home requires trust and teamwork, not only bricks and mortar.
- Shared community background may earn family approval, yet shared values and goals drive genuine partnership.

Relying exclusively on these metrics creates blind spots. Quick tempers, poor communication habits, and cruelty under stress can remain invisible until after the wedding.

Section 2: Emotional Intelligence: The Overlooked Essential

Emotional intelligence (EQ) is the ability to recognize, understand, and manage one's own emotions and those of others. In the context of marriage, high EQ enables:

- Healthy conflict resolution: "I feel hurt when you do this," not blame and defensiveness.
- Empathy and attunement, noticing a partner's distress and responding before resentment builds.
- Clear boundaries, managing in-law involvement and outside interference without drama.

A partner who responds to every disagreement with silence or aggression creates loneliness, regardless of their wealth. No bank balance compensates for a heart that feels perpetually unheard.

Section 3: Case Study, Wealth Without Compatibility

Arjun & Priya

On paper, this match was ideal: Arjun ran a tech start-up with a six-figure income; Priya led a successful marketing team; both families commanded community respect.

Yet their marriage collapsed within two years. Arjun shut down whenever Priya raised concerns; Priya responded with guilt-tripping. He prioritized late-night work sessions; she felt abandoned. Neither had a framework for emotional care.

Minor frictions hardened into deep resentments, and they divorced, each feeling they had personally failed, when in reality they had simply never been equipped with the tools to succeed.

The lesson is clear: compatibility requires deliberate emotional effort, not merely compatible pedigrees.

Section 4: Guided Reflection, Identify Your Blind Spots

Reflective Prompts

1. What qualities do I list first when imagining an ideal partner?
2. How do I handle anger, do I talk it through or shut down?
3. Have I ever asked a prospective partner about their core values and beliefs?
4. How would I respond if my partner earned significantly less than me?
5. Do I lean on family status or social approval to resolve my own doubts about a match?

Fixating on wealth, property, or family name creates a blind spot that conceals a person's true capacity to love, support, and grow with another. Emotional intelligence and shared values are the bedrock of a lasting union. By identifying your blind spots now, you protect yourself from avoidable pain later. The next chapter explores how to build emotional skills and recognize a partner whose inner qualities, not merely whose credentials, will genuinely elevate your life.

CHAPTER 3

The Crisis Across Genders: Hidden Wounds and Silent Harms

Every year, thousands of brides die under dowry-related pressure. Thousands of husbands end their lives following false legal accusations. These tragedies share a common root: a broken system that traps both men and women in a spiral of silent suffering, stigma, and despair.

Women's Hidden Ordeal: Dowry Harassment and Abuse

Dowry harassment rarely begins with open violence. It typically starts quictly, small requests, minor insults, and escalates over time into threats and physical harm.

Common Signs of Dowry Harassment

- Repeated demands for cash, jewellery, or property
- Verbal abuse and public humiliation when demands go unmet
- Deliberate isolation from family and friends

- Threats of abandonment, divorce, or further violence

Psychological Impact

- Persistent anxiety and anticipatory fear
- Deep depression and a pervasive sense of hopelessness
- Erosion of self-confidence and self-identity
- Feeling trapped with no visible path to safety

Case Example, Sita's Struggle

Sita married into a well-established household. On her wedding day, her in-laws requested a car. When her parents could not provide it, daily insults began. Doors were locked.

She was cut off from relatives who might have helped. Sita stopped eating and cried alone each night, her pleas unheard.

Men's Hidden Ordeal: False Accusations and Legal Misuse

Societal narratives have historically centred female victimhood; men, too, face a silent and deeply under-acknowledged crisis. Weaponized legal complaints can strip a man of his home, his children, and his professional standing before a single hearing.

Warning Signs of Legal Coercion

- Sudden filing of domestic violence or harassment complaints coinciding with divorce negotiations
- Threats to "ruin" a career unless financial demands are met
- Blocking access to children as a tactical maneuver
- Social media campaigns designed to damage reputation before a case is heard

Case Example, Raj's Ordeal

Raj, a schoolteacher, was served with an emergency protective order one morning, barring him from his home and his two children. No prior warning was given. Within days, colleagues and neighbours had heard the news.

Weeks later, his wife admitted in mediation that she had exaggerated allegations during an acrimonious financial dispute. Raj's reputation and mental health suffered damage that lingered long after the case was dismissed.

Universal Warning Signs in Matrimonial Disputes

Regardless of gender, the following patterns warrant immediate attention:

- Escalating financial demands or threats

- Legal or social pressure deployed as a control mechanism
- Deliberate isolation from support networks

Recommended Steps

1. Speak to a trusted friend, counsellor, or legal professional without delay.
2. Document all incidents, communications, and financial transactions in writing.
3. Research local support organizations available to both men and women.
4. Seek qualified legal advice before disputes escalate further.

The experiences of Anita, Vikram, Sita, and Raj are not isolated incidents, they are symptoms of a system that pressures both men and women into silence, despair, and, in the worst cases, tragedy. Marital trauma does not discriminate by gender. It thrives on unspoken expectations and broken promises. We must break this cycle: speak out when you witness unfair demands or false threats, and support those who feel trapped.

The next chapter examines how inter-generational control within families compounds these crises, and what can be done about it.

CHAPTER 4

In-Law Enmeshment: Boundary Battles and Loss of Intimacy

Imagine waking before dawn to prepare breakfast, only to find your new mother-in-law examining every spice jar on the shelf, dismissing your approach as inexperienced. In that moment, you step into what this chapter calls the In-Law Matrix, a web of cultural expectations, loyalty obligations, and unspoken control mechanisms that can quietly smother a couple's private world.

The In-Law Matrix

In many traditions, marriage extends beyond two individuals to bind entire families. Joint households celebrate unity and shared resources, but they also blur personal boundaries. Common manifestations of the In-Law Matrix include:

- Unannounced daily visits framed as "family bonding."
- Veto power by elders over household purchases, décor, or child-rearing.
- Implicit cultural scripts declaring that parents "know best," making boundary-setting feel disrespectful.
- Emotional leverage: couples feel disloyal or guilty if they request privacy.

Both partners become ensnared. A husband raised in a close-knit family may feel he dishonors his mother by protecting his privacy. A wife socialized to defer to elders may fear the label of "disrespectful daughter-in-law." Over time, these small concessions calcify into a rigid framework that undermines the couple's autonomy and mutual trust.

Erosion of Intimacy

When the In-Law Matrix takes hold, intimacy erodes gradually but relentlessly. Privacy violations become routine:

- A mother-in-law listens in on conversations "to help."
- A father-in-law reads private messages "out of concern."
- Extended family members comment publicly on the couple's relationship.

These incursions trigger a damaging cycle:

- Intrusion: an in-law steps into a personal discussion uninvited.
- Withdrawal: one partner shuts down to avoid exposure.
- Resentment: the other partner is blamed for failing to protect the space.
- Further intrusion: elders intervene again, convinced "the couple needs guidance."

Gradually, intimate conversations about finances, fears, and dreams give way to curt exchanges or silence. The couple become housemates united by circumstance rather than connection.

Case Study, Rahul and Priya

Rahul's mother moved in two weeks after the wedding "to help Priya settle in." Two weeks became two months. Priya endured constant scrutiny of her cooking, her cleaning routines, and her decorating choices. Rahul, torn between filial loyalty and care for his wife, avoided confrontation.

Private conversations migrated to the bathroom; laughter disappeared. After a minor argument erupted in front of the extended family, both partners sought couples counselling.

In therapy they identified three core problems: no defined timeline for the in-law stay, no private zone within the home, and an absence of early negotiation.

Together they drafted enforceable guest rules, a firm departure date, two uninterrupted evening hours for the couple, and a private home-office space off-limits to all guests. Within days, warmth returned to their conversations and their home became a sanctuary once more.

Reflective Prompts

1. Which in-law behaviors feel most invasive in your relationship?
2. On a scale of 1 to 10, how safe do you feel sharing personal concerns in front of extended family?
3. List three areas you want to keep strictly between you and your partner, finances, health, relationship concerns.
4. Draft one boundary statement using an "I" message: "I feel overwhelmed when..."
5. When will you schedule a calm, private conversation with your partner to agree on boundaries?

In-law enmeshment need not doom a marriage. By recognizing the In-Law Matrix, understanding how privacy violations erode emotional closeness, and drawing on the example of couples like Rahul and Priya, you can equip yourselves with the clarity and courage to draw protective lines. Boundaries are not fortress walls; they are guardrails that preserve the space in which your relationship can flourish. The next chapter explores constructive strategies for conflict resolution with parents, transforming clashes into opportunities for deeper mutual understanding.

CHAPTER 5

Weaponized Statutes: Legal Warfare and Systemic Trauma

Protective laws, domestic violence statutes, emergency restraining orders, custody provisions, were forged through decades of courageous advocacy. Their original purpose was unambiguous: save lives, restore dignity, and affirm every person's right to a violence-free home. This chapter examines how that framework can be misused as a strategic weapon in divorce and custody disputes, and what the human cost of that misuse looks like.

Protective Laws and Their Original Intent

From the 1970s onward, survivor advocates, legal reformers, and social activists united to demand clear legal tools against spousal abuse. Legislators responded with low-threshold "reasonable belief" standards for emergency orders and mandatory arrest policies. Family courts, once reluctant to intervene in "private" disputes, began granting swift relief: temporary custody transfers, exclusive use of the marital home, and interim financial support. The unifying purpose was both moral and pragmatic, stop abuse before it escalates, prevent further trauma, and give the vulnerable a path to safety.

Tactical Misuse

The same low evidentiary threshold that protects genuine victims can, in some hands, be weaponized. A single police call or affidavit of fear can trigger an emergency order, remove a spouse from their home, and suspend parental contact, all before the accused has had a day in court.

False allegations frequently accompany coercive divorce negotiations. A partner seeking a disproportionate financial settlement may threaten to allege abuse unless demands are met. Faced with the prospect of arrest, media exposure, and prolonged legal proceedings, many capitulate. Countersuits, claims of financial control, accusations of parental alienation, further transform protective statutes into bargaining chips rather than safety nets.

The consequences are severe. Wrongfully accused individuals endure shattered reputations, financial ruin from legal costs, and lasting psychological harm. Genuine victims, meanwhile, hesitate to seek help, fearing their accounts will be dismissed or tainted by association with fabricated claims.

Courtroom Stories: Three Faces of Misuse

Alex's Unwanted Exile

Alex, a dedicated engineer and father of two, was blindsided when his estranged wife secured an emergency protective order. Without prior warning, he was removed from their shared home and denied weekend contact with his children.

Neighbours whispered; his employment contract was jeopardized. Weeks later, the charges were withdrawn, his former wife acknowledged she had exaggerated claims during an acrimonious alimony dispute. The professional and psychological damage Alex sustained proved far more enduring than the order itself.

Maya's Compromised Victory

Maya had endured years of psychological abuse and physical threats. She documented every incident meticulously, photographs, therapy notes, message records.

When she finally sought a restraining order, the court initially hesitated: her ex produced superficial counter-evidence and accused her of fabricating communications. After two grueling hearings, Maya secured full protection.

But the delay left her isolated in a shelter far from her workplace, and the prolonged ordeal extended her trauma well beyond the final judgment.

Ravi's Silent Struggle

Ravi, trapped in a coerced arranged marriage, endured verbal and financial abuse for years before filing for divorce.

His former wife then alleged that routine social media activity constituted harassment, and an order was issued barring Ravi from his home and children. Only a vigorous defense, multiple character witnesses, and an extended evidentiary hearing cleared his name.

By then, he had nearly lost custody of his young child, and his professional prospects had been irreparably damaged.

Reflective Prompts

1. When might a protective statute cross the line from legitimate shield to punitive weapon? Identify three warning signs.
2. If a friend confided that they were experiencing legal coercion, what concrete steps would you recommend?

3. Propose two reforms, legislative or procedural, that could balance urgent protection with safeguards against misuse.

4. Reflect honestly: do you hold unconscious biases that favor the accuser or the accused in abuse claims?

5. How might legal advocates and therapists collaborate to distinguish genuine risk from tactical misuse?

Protective statutes emerged from a collective determination to end domestic violence and shield families from harm. Their power lies in swift intervention and moral clarity. But when misapplied as instruments of legal warfare, they inflict systemic trauma as severe as the abuse they were designed to prevent.

Understanding their original intent, recognizing coercive tactics, and hearing real courtroom narratives gives every reader the knowledge to navigate these laws ethically, preserving protection for those who genuinely need it while safeguarding fairness for all.

CHAPTER 6

The “Log Kya Kahenge” Epidemic: The Tyranny of Social Stigma

"Log kya kahenge", "What will people say?", is perhaps the most powerful unspoken force in the Indian matrimonial landscape.

It shapes decisions, silences victims, and keeps toxic relationships intact long past the point of repair. This chapter dissects the anatomy of social stigma, traces its grip on individual lives, and offers a path toward reclaiming your voice.

The Anatomy of Gossip

Gossip travels through three primary channels in Indian social life:

- Word-of-mouth networks, relatives, neighbours, and family friends. One mother's concern about her son's late arrival can become an accusation of infidelity within hours.
- Digital wildfire, a screenshot, an off-hand comment, a manipulated image. Social media accelerates rumor exponentially, each retelling adding fresh distortions.

- The role of bystanders, most gossip is shared out of curiosity or misplaced loyalty, with no awareness of the reputational damage it leaves in its wake.

Understanding how gossip spreads gives us the tools to resist it. Pausing before we share, questioning our sources, and choosing empathy over sensationalism are the first acts of resistance.

Social Stigma's Grip

The fear of being talked about translates into a fear of living authentically:

- Ostracism and shame, even a hint of marital discord can trigger exclusion from community ceremonies, keeping many silent in the face of abuse.
- Control through izzat (honor), family reputation is social currency. Actions perceived as tarnishing it invite withdrawal of support, public reprimand, or arranged "damage-control" marriages.
- Silencing the victim, a battered spouse is told, "Don't ruin the family name." A struggling child is told, "Suffer in silence." Both messages rank societal validation above personal safety.

When stigma wields this power, mental health deteriorates. Anxiety, depression, and suicidal ideation emerge behind closed doors, concealed by forced smiles and rehearsed explanations.

Case Studies: Stigma-Driven Tragedies

Ayesha's Silent Scream

Ayesha married at twenty-two, full of optimism. When her husband's anger turned physical, she begged her parents to intervene. Their response: "Don't talk about it.

What will the relatives think?" Day after day, she endured bruises in the name of family honor. She tried to contact a helpline but feared the consequences if the call were discovered.

Three weeks later, she was gone, her death attributed in hushed tones to "bad luck" rather than to the societal failure it represented.

Rohit's Invisible Battle

Rohit, thirty, confided to friends that he felt trapped in an unloving arranged marriage. He wanted a divorce and professional counselling. His parents strongly discouraged both, genuinely fearing the social shame they believed it would bring the family. "Divorce brings shame," they said.

Pressured to stay, Rohit's depression deepened until he was admitted to a psychiatric ward. Only then did his family accept that mental health is as vital as reputation. By the time the stigma was lifted, Rohit had lost years of relationships and self-esteem.

Reflective Prompts

1. Recall a time you remained silent to protect your family's reputation. What feelings did that choice produce?
2. Identify one rumor, or fear of rumor, that has shaped your decisions. How would your life look without that fear?
3. List three concrete ways you can support someone in your community who is facing shame or gossip.
4. What would you tell a younger sibling about choosing personal well-being over societal validation?
5. Visualize life beyond stigma: what relationships and opportunities could flourish if you refused to yield?

The tyranny of social stigma thrives on silence and compliance. But every time we challenge a rumor, speak out about injustice, or choose self-respect over reputation management, we erode its power. Breaking the Log Kya Kahenge epidemic means placing human life above hollow social validation, forging communities where honesty and compassion take precedence over judgment. Make a promise today: you will not let gossip define your choices, shame dictate your future, or silence cost you your life.

CHAPTER 7

Breaking Free: Cultivating Healthy Boundaries and Choices

Every journey toward healing begins with a single act of courage: saying no. You may stand at a crossroads, burdened by unspoken expectations, families insisting on tradition, partners imposing hidden rules, society demanding conformity. But boundaries are not walls to keep love out; they are bridges to self-respect, autonomy, and lasting peace. This chapter equips you to spot warning signs of control, communicate with clarity and compassion, draw strength from those who have walked this path, and build a personal action plan to reclaim your agency.

Identifying Red Flags

Psychological Warning Signs

When manipulation hides behind warmth, it can be almost invisible. Watch for:

- Gaslighting: "You're overreacting" or "That never happened."
- Guilt-tripping: "After everything I have sacrificed, you cannot do this one thing for me?"

- Emotional withholding: using silence, stonewalling, or affection as a weapon or reward.

If you find yourself constantly apologizing for "being difficult" or doubting your own memory, these are red flags that demand attention.

Financial Warning Signs

Money frequently serves as a proxy for power. Be alert to:

- Hidden debts or undisclosed accounts controlled unilaterally by a partner or family member.
- Pressure to sign contracts or transfer assets without adequate time to consult a professional.
- A refusal to share financial information or discuss budgets openly.

A genuine partnership shares both responsibility and transparency.

Behavioral Warning Signs

Actions reveal intent more reliably than words. Notice whether someone:

- Monitors your calls, messages, or social media without consent.
- Isolates you from friends or personal interests under the guise of "family unity."

- Coerces major decisions, living arrangements, career moves, wedding plans, through relentless pressure.

Boundary-Setting Strategies

Communication Techniques

- I-statements: "I feel overwhelmed when decisions are made without my input."
- Broken-record technique: calmly repeat your boundary, even under sustained pushback.
- Time-outs: "I need twenty-four hours to consider this before we continue the conversation."

These tools shift dynamics from conflict to collaboration, articulating your needs without blame.

Self-Advocacy Practices

- Clarify non-negotiables: financial independence, alone time, personal growth.
- Schedule regular self-check-ins: journaling, walks, or therapy sessions.
- Build an ally network: identify friends, mentors, or professionals who honor your boundaries.

Real-Life Success Stories

Financial Freedom Together, Sara and Amir

Sara and Amir discovered that their engagement came with an unexpected condition: his parents expected to control their joint account.

Rather than capitulating or creating conflict, they calmly presented a co-ownership plan linked to their shared financial goals. They regained autonomy while earning family trust rather than inheriting family control.

Digital Privacy, Emotional Security, Diego and Priya

Priya's mother demanded access to the couple's private group chat. Priya responded with an I-statement: "I appreciate your concern, but our private space helps us grow as a couple." Her steady, respectful resolve eventually led to genuine mutual respect and healthier involvement from her mother.

Community Expectations vs. Personal Pace, Leila

Leila's traditional family pressured her to start a family immediately after marriage. She set a clear boundary: "I cherish our future, but I need two years to build my career and my personal well-being first." Her honest timeline earned respect and preserved her mental health, strengthening relationships rather than fraying them.

Reflective Prompts

1. Which psychological, financial, or behavioral warning signs resonate most with your experience?
2. List at least five personal boundaries you refuse to compromise on.
3. Complete and practice aloud: "I need _______ because _______."
4. Name three people you can contact when you need reinforcement or accountability.
5. What is your first milestone this week toward communicating one boundary clearly?

Breaking free is not a single dramatic moment, it is a continuous commitment to your own well-being. Every line you draw, every "no" you speak, reaffirms your worth and fortifies your peace. As you practice these strategies and refine your action plan, you will discover that healthy boundaries do not close people off; they create the safety within which deeper, more authentic connection becomes possible. Carry this roadmap with you as you step into the final chapter of your journey, one defined not by external demands, but by your own values, choices, and unwavering self-respect.

CHAPTER 8

Toward Intentional Partnerships: Transforming Traditions

Imagine a world where the art of matchmaking feels not like a transaction but like a conscious collaboration between two individuals and their families. For centuries, Indian traditions have guided unions through caste considerations, horoscope compatibility, and community expectations. While these customs carry genuine wisdom, many no longer serve the emotional needs of contemporary couples. Transforming tradition begins with a single shift: understanding marriage not as compliance with inherited norms, but as a partnership built on mutual consent and deep compatibility.

Redefining Marriage Traditions

Modern frameworks for assessing compatibility focus on three dimensions:

- Core values, beliefs about family, spirituality, career, and personal ethics.
- Life goals, plans for children, living arrangements, and financial priorities.

- Emotional needs, communication styles, conflict approaches, and intimacy preferences.

> **Aisha and Rahul**
>
> *Their families arranged an introduction based on community ties. Rather than passively following horoscope compatibility scores, they engaged in deliberate conversations guided by a values inventory.*
>
> *They discovered shared entrepreneurial dreams, mutual respect for each other's family bonds, and complementary approaches to difficult conversations. By applying a modern framework, they transformed tradition into a scaffold for genuine connection.*

From Compliance to Consent

Too often, young adults feel obligated to obey parental marriage preferences. Compliance means saying yes because elders asked.

Consent means choosing a partner based on personal agency and self-awareness. Cultivating this agency involves three practices:

Self-Reflection Journaling

- "What qualities matter most to me in a partner, and why?"

- "Which inherited assumptions about marriage no longer align with my vision?"

Boundary-Setting Conversations

- Role-play negotiating dating timelines or family involvement expectations.
- Use I-statements: "I feel ready to commit when..." or "I need your support around..."

Inner Alliance Exercises

- Visualize your adult self holding space for your younger self's hopes and fears.
- Acknowledge emotional blocks, fear of disappointing family or losing cultural connection.

Priya's Journey

Priya felt torn between honoring her parents' wishes and pursuing her own path. Through weekly journaling and respectful family dialogues, she moved from acquiescence ("Yes, I'll meet him") to informed consent ("I choose to explore this relationship, and here is why"). She found her voice, and so can you.

Planning Intentional Partnerships

Intentional partnerships do not happen by accident. They require structured tools:

- Values Inventory Worksheet, list your top five personal values and rate a prospective partner's alignment on a 1–5 scale.
- Non-Negotiable Criteria, identify deal-breakers and distinguish them from flexible preferences.
- Shared Vision Map, create a Venn diagram of "Your goals," "My goals," and "Our goals," then discuss discrepancies and creative compromises.

Pre-Marital Conversation Prompts

- Money: spending versus saving habits, debt management, financial independence.
- Family involvement: frequency of visits, caregiving responsibilities, decision-making authority.
- Conflict style: agreed time-out signals, apology languages, repair rituals.
- Growth plan: individual development goals and how you will support each other in pursuing them.

Encouraging Parental Evolution

Parents also undergo transformation, from matchmakers enforcing tradition to mentors supporting autonomy. Strategies to facilitate this shift include:

- Perspective-Taking Exercises, parents list their hopes for their child's marriage; the child does the same. Swap lists and reflect without judgment.
- Active Listening Practice, mirror back what you heard: "You are concerned about..." Validate feelings before offering advice.
- Family Dialogue Framework, set a shared agenda; use timed speaking turns to ensure every voice is heard.
- Guided Mediation Sessions, an impartial facilitator helps navigate sensitive topics: caste concerns, financial arrangements, in-law expectations.

The Patel Family

Mr. and Mrs. Patel were determined to preserve cultural values; their son Anand felt suffocated by rigid rules.

Through a series of structured family dialogues and empathy exercises, they discovered common ground: a shared respect for heritage and a shared desire for Anand's happiness.

Parents learned to ask open-ended questions rather than issue directives. In this new dynamic, every voice, including Anand's, mattered.

Your Final Reflective Roadmap

Reflective Prompts

1. List three traditions you value. Can they be reframed to support personal agency rather than compliance?
2. How do you define consent in the context of your own life and relationships?
3. Complete your Values Inventory Worksheet and draft your Non-Negotiable Criteria list.
4. Schedule one active-listening session with a parent or family elder this week.
5. At one-month intervals, revisit this roadmap and note shifts in understanding, areas of tension, and successes.

Traditions can guide us without binding us. Intentional partnerships thrive when individuals and families embrace emotional intelligence, open communication, and a genuinely shared vision. Use the tools in this chapter to spark meaningful dialogue, cultivate personal agency, and build a marriage that honors the wisdom of the past while pioneering a future defined by consent, compatibility, and mutual growth. Your journey toward a conscious, joyous union begins here.

About the Author

Muskan Sharma is a dedicated first-generation advocate practicing before the Hon'ble Punjab and Haryana High Court.

She holds a B.Com LLB and an LLM, and is currently advancing her expertise as a PhD Scholar. Based in SAS Nagar (Mohali), Punjab, Muskan has extensive hands-on experience in family law, having successfully handled and provided counsel in numerous complex matrimonial cases and domestic disputes.

Beyond her legal practice, she is a committed social changemaker and an active member of Seva Bharti. Through this work she contributes to a vast network of community service projects across India, supporting over five thousand healthcare centers, free and subsidized education for underprivileged children, critical disaster relief operations, and the economic empowerment of self-employed women.

Driven by a passion for justice and community welfare, Muskan combines rigorous academic training with real-world legal advocacy to uplift the most vulnerable members of society.

www.ingramcontent.com/pod-product-compliance
Lightning Source LLC
LaVergne TN
LVHW022031200926
848481LV00007B/2639